60 POSITIVE ACTIVITIES FOR KIDS

CREATED BY
TERESA X. NGUYEN

ILLUSTRATED BY
TYLER HOANG

Country of Manufacture Specified on Last Page
First Printing 2019

1. The Best Things in Life Are Free

Related Topics

Holidays, Shopping, Friends and Family

Sample Language

I love sunny weather.

My family is the best thing in life.

You can't buy friends in a store.

Suggested Prompts

What do you think "the best things in life" means?

What are some things that are free?

What makes you happy? Are they things you can't buy in a store?

2. Quick Ways to Make me Laugh

Related Topics

Jokes and Humor, Hobbies, Emotions

Sample Language

It's funny when …

I always laugh when …

My favorite joke is …

… movie is so funny.

Suggested Prompts

Do you know any funny jokes?

What are some funny things your friends do?

Do you ever do silly things for fun?

Do you like funny movies or TV shows or books?

3. Thank you note to someone who helped you recently.

Related Topics

Thanksgiving, Writing Letters, Friends and Family

Sample Language

Dear …

Sincerely …

Thank you for …

I am grateful because …

It was nice of you to …

Suggested Prompts

Who are some people who help you?

When was the last time someone helped you?

What are some big or small things people have done for you lately?

4. A funny photo

Related Topics

Famous Places, Tourism, Friends and Family

Sample Language

This is my friend …

I took this photo at …

It was spring of 2022.

Last year, I went …

Suggested Prompts

Can you think of a funny scene you saw?

What's the funniest TV show or movie you know?

Can you think of someone you know who is always doing silly things?

What's a funny scene you can imagine?

5. What Would Your Planet Look Like?

Related Topics

Environment, Space, Geography, Famous Places

Sample Language

My planet has lots of …

There are no … because I don't like them.

See this island? That's where the … live.

It is always sunny on this continent.

Suggested Prompts

What kind of environment do you like?

What's your favorite planet?

What would your ideal planet have on it?

If you could live anywhere in the world, where would you live? Why?

6. Dream Home

Related Topics

Houses and Home, Everyday Activities, Hobbies

Sample Language

The living room has a big swimming pool in it.

There's a video game room here.

My kitchen has …

The bedroom is next to the library.

Suggested Prompts

What are your favorite rooms in your house?

Have you ever seen a TV show about rich and famous people's houses?

What do you do for fun?

Where do you like to go for vacation? What do you do there?

7. My Advice About Life

Related Topics

Values and Beliefs, Giving Advice

Sample Language

My dad always says …

Everyone should …

Never …

Suggested Prompts

Do your parents give you good advice?

Do you have a secret to life?

What is something you are good at? How did you get good at it?

8. Silly Jokes I Know

Related Topics

Jokes and Humor, Entertainment

Sample Language

So this guy is walking down the street …

There's a rabbit in the woods …

What do you call a …

Suggested Prompts

What are some of your favorite jokes?

What's your favorite funny movie or TV show or book? What are the funniest parts?

What kinds of jokes do you like?

What's the last joke you heard?

9. A New Food Creation

Related Topics

Food, Holidays

Sample Language

It's made from …

There are noodles.

It tastes very sweet/sour/bitter/savory.

Suggested Prompts

What's your favorite food? What is in it?

What are some foods you think would taste good together?

What's the most unusual meal you ever ate? What was in it?

10. I Laughed So Hard When …

Related Topics

Jokes and Humor, Entertainment, Emotions

Sample Language

Yesterday, I saw something funny.

Once my friend …

Something that made me laugh was when …

My brother always makes me laugh when he …

Suggested Prompts

What are some funny things your friends do?

When was the last time you laughed? What happened?

What's the funniest movie or TV show you've ever seen?

11. A Dream That Came True

Related Topics

Dreams, Goals and Ambitions

Sample Language

I had a dream where …

In my dream, I was …

Then, I realized …

Suggested Prompts

Have you ever had a dream that came true?

What's something you dreamed about, then it came true?

Have you ever had a good dream and you wish it came true?

12. Colors That Make You Happy

Related Topics

Colors, Emotions

Sample Language

My favorite color is …

When I see blue, I think of …

The color red reminds me of …

Green is the color of …

Suggested Prompts

What's your favorite color?

What feelings do different colors make you feel?

Do certain colors remind you of something?

If you could be any color, which one would you choose?

13. A Happy Message in The Sky

Related Topics

Giving Advice

Sample Language

If I could put a message in the sky, it would say …

I would like a message that says …

My message to the world is …

Suggested Prompts

What's some advice you would give to everyone in the world?

What is a message that makes you feel happy?

What is something your friends or family always say to make you feel better when you're sad?

14. What Is Your Favorite Memory?

Related Topics

Narratives, Memories

Sample Language

I remember when …

One memory I treasure is when …

It all started when …

This happened three years ago.

Suggested Prompts

When did you last smile?

What's the most exciting thing you've ever done?

Did you ever have a great vacation?

Have you ever seen something unusual?

15. Good Things I've Done Big Or Small

Related Topics

About Myself, Goals

Sample Language

I'm proud of myself for …

One good thing I've done is …

This is a small thing, but I'm proud that I …

Suggested Prompts

What's the biggest you've ever done?

What's something you are proud of?

What's something you've done that no one knows about?

What's something you are good at?

16. Selfie

Related Topics

About Me, Describing People, Everyday Activities, Hobbies

Sample Language

This is me. I drew my hair like this because …

This is my favorite shirt. I like it because …

I'm holding a ball because …

In this picture, I'm at … because …

In real life, my eyes are blue, but I drew them green because …

Suggested Prompts

What's your favorite part of your face or body?

What's your favorite outfit?

What hobbies do you enjoy?

Do you ever want to change anything about yourself?

17. The People of My Life

Related Topics

Friends and Family, Describing People

Sample Language

This is my dad/mom/sister/brother …

… is my best friend. I like him because …

I've known … for 2 years.

My cousin is special because …

Suggested Prompts

Who are the people in your family?

Who are your best friends?

What's your favorite thing about your family members and your friends?

Is there someone close to you?

18. I Am Special Because …

Related Topics

About Me, Describing People,

Sample Language

I really like that I can …

I'm good at …

My friends say I'm …

My mom likes that I …

Suggested Prompts

What's something you are good at?

What's something you are proud of?

Is there something people compliment you on a lot?

19. A Present to Myself

Related Topics

Holidays, Birthdays, Shopping

Sample Language

If I could get myself a present, I would buy …

I've always wanted a …

I love stuffed animals, so I would get myself a …

I wish I were good at …

Suggested Prompts

What is something you've always wanted? Why?

If you had a million dollars, what would you buy? Why?

What are some things you need that can't be bought in a store?

20. An Enjoyable Conversation

Related Topics

Narratives, Small Talk

Sample Language

This happened last spring.

He told me …

She said, "…"

I laughed when he said that.

Suggested Prompts

When was the last time you talked to a friend?

What do you talk about to your friends?

What does your family like to talk about?

21. The Future is in Your Hands

Related Topics

The Future, Goals

Sample Language

You will …

You are going to …

Suggested Prompts

What do you hope happens to you in the future?

What's a prediction you have for your friends?

Have you ever gotten an interesting fortune from a fortune cookie?

22. Create Your Own Movie

Related Topics

Movies and entertainment

Sample Language

My movie is about …

The main character is a …

So in the end,

Suggested Prompts

What kind of movies do you like?

Are you good at making up stories?

What's a movie you like that no one else likes?

23. #1 Song

Related Topics

Entertainment, Poetry

Sample Language

varies

Suggested Prompts

What are some of your favorite songs?

What are your favorite lyrics from songs you like?

What are some different songs you like that are about the same theme?

What are some different songs that make you feel the same way?

Do you know any songs that are so similar you sometimes mix up the words?

24. What Is Your Happy Smell?

Related Topics

About You, Food, Holidays

Sample Language

I love the smell of …

My favorite smell is … because it reminds me of …

It has a sweet smell …

It's kind of flowery.

When I smell it, I think of …

Suggested Prompts

What's your favorite food? What does it smell like?

Do you like incense or scented candles?

Do you have a favorite perfume or scented soap?

What does your house or the house of a friend or family member smell like?

25. A Rule Everyone Should Follow

Related Topics

Giving Advice, School, Work, Society, Politics, Government, Law

Sample Language

Always …

Never …

Try …

If you don't …, you won't …

Suggested Prompts

What piece of advice do you think everyone should listen to?

What is something you wish everyone would do at school or at work or in your home?

What's a behavior that people do that makes you upset or annoyed?

What's a law or policy you think makes the world a better place?

What's something you value and think is important in the world?

26. Congratulations To Me

Related Topics

School, Work, Goals

Sample Language

Congratulations to me for …

I should be congratulated for …

I'm proud that I …

I can't believe I …

Suggested Prompts

What's a goal you achieved recently?

What's something you worked very hard to do or get?

What's an achievement that you wish more people knew about?

When was the last time someone said congratulations to you?

27. #Thankful

Related Topics

Friends and Family, Thanksgiving

Sample Language

1. … do a cool dance from social media.

2. … my problems.

3. … helps me do my homework.

4. … takes care of me.

5. … always makes me laugh.

6. … shares their snacks with me.

Suggested Prompts

Who are some people who help you?

What are some things your friends or family are good at it?

Who is someone that you can always talk to?

Who is someone that you are always happy to see?

28. Souvenirs From the Adventures I've Been on

Related Topics

Tourism, Travel, Goals

Sample Language

This is a book I got in Australia.

I saw this cool rock on a hike last year.

This toy Statue of Liberty is from my trip to New York.

My friend and I explored a swamp in our backyard this weekend. I drew some cattails to remember that.

Suggested Prompts

What are some places you visited?

What are some things you got from vacations or trips?

Have you done something fun? Can you draw something that reminds you of it?

29. I'm Happy When

Related Topics

Emotions

Sample Language

… I see my friends.

… someone says something nice to me.

… the weather is nice.

… I play baseball.

… I get good grades.

Suggested Prompts

What are your favorite holidays? What makes you happy on those days?

What are your favorite activities? What do you like about them?

Do you have a favorite time of year?

Do you have a favorite place?

30. All the Places I Hope to Visit One Day

Related Topics

Tourism, Travel, Geography

Sample Language

I want to go to Barcelona because I hear the buildings are cool.

I hope I go to Italy this year. My grandma lives there.

I think Jamaica has great beaches.

I'd like to see the Grand Canyon.

Suggested Prompts

Where would you go if you could

do anywhere in the world?

What's a place that a friend went to and loved?

What are some famous places you want to see for yourself?

What's a place you want to go to that most people have never heard of?

31. Some New Emotions

Related Topics

Emotions, Describing People

Sample Language

This face means …

It's a smiley face but the eyes are musical notes …

I love the feeling when you read a book that reminds you of another book.

The feeling of eating Smores at a campfire needs a new emotion called …

Suggested Prompts

What's an emotion you feel that doesn't have a name?

Is there a feeling your culture that doesn't have a word in English?

What's your favorite emoji?

32. Random Memory with Someone I Love

Related Topics

Narratives

Sample Language

I'll never forget …

This happened 2 years ago …

I met my best friend in 2021.

This was the most fun day ever!

Suggested Prompts

What's one of your happiest memories? Who were you with and what did you do?

What's one of your weirdest memo-

ries? Who were you with and what did you do?

Is there a memory that always makes you think of a certain person?

Is there a person in your life that always reminds you of a special day?

33. New Holiday

Related Topics

Holidays, Celebrations, Travel

Sample Language

My new holiday is Pizza for Breakfast Day.

On Picnic Day, everyone has to go outside and have a picnic.

I think there should be a holiday for Katherine Goble Johnson, a black female mathematician who worked at NASA.

The way you celebrate this holiday is to …

On this holiday, people will eat …

Suggested Prompts

What is a person or event you think deserves a holiday to remember?

What is an activity or thing you think deserves a holiday so everyone can celebrate it?

Are there any holidays that people celebrate in other countries that you want to celebrate too?

What are some ways to celebrate your holiday? Do people eat special foods? Do special activities? Go to a certain place?

34. Recent Moments of Joy

Related Topics

Emotions

Sample Language

Recently, I had a really fun experience.

This was a small thing, but it made

me happy.

This was a cool thing that happened the other day …

Suggested Prompts

When's the last time something made you happy?

How many times have you felt joy this week?

Is there something in your house, at work, or in school that always makes you feel good when you see it?

35. The Best Vacation

Related Topics

Travel, Tourism, Geography

Sample Language

The best place I've ever gone is …

They eat … there. It's so good because …

You can go … there.

There are beautiful plants and animals there …

Suggested Prompts

What's the best vacation you've ever been on? Where did you go and what was it like?

What's a place you would love to travel to? What would you do there?

Imagine the perfect place to go on vacation, even if it isn't a real place, and describe it.

36. My Hero Vs. Me

Related Topics

People, Heroes

Sample Language

My hero is Superman and both of us are …

Compared to my hero, I'm more …

Unlike me, my hero is …

Someday I hope to be … too.

Suggested Prompts

Who are some of your heroes? What do you admire about them?

In what ways are you like your heroes?

In what ways are you different?

If there was one quality you could improve to be more like your hero, what would it be?

What is one quality about yourself that reminds you of your hero?

37. Music Playlist

Related Topics

Music, Entertainment, About Me, Hobbies

Sample Language

I love this song because …

I really like rock music.

I'm not a fan of pop, but I do like …

My favorite band is …

One song I can't live without is …

I must listen to … every day.

Suggested Prompts

What are some of your favorite songs?

What's your favorite band? What kind of music do they play?

Is there a kind of music that always makes you happy?

Are there songs that make you dance?

38. Compliments I've Received

Related Topics

About Me

Sample Language

A lot of people say I'm …

Once my mom told me …

"You're very good at …"

"You have wonderful taste in …"

Suggested Prompts

What is something people often compliment you on?

Is there something a teacher told you?

What is your family proud of about you?

39. The Most Beautiful Thing I've Seen

Related Topics

Tourism, The Environment, Shopping

Sample Language

It took my breath away.

It was so beautiful that I …

It was made of …

It looked like …

Suggested Prompts

What's the most beautiful scenery you've ever seen?

Do you have a favorite piece of art?

Have you ever seen something beautiful in a store?

40. Fun Words to Say

Related Topics

Language, Literature

Sample Language

Varies

Suggested Prompts

What are your favorite words in English?

Are there any words you like the sound of?

Do you use a word just because of how it sounds?

Do you know any nonsense words?

41. Design Your T-Shirt for Each Day of the Week

Related Topics

Clothes, Shopping, Art

Sample Language

I have Taekwondo practice on Mondays, so I would wear ….

My Tuesday T-shirt has rainbows because …

I love blue, so all my T-shirts have blue on them.

Thursday, I'd wear a T-shirt with my favorite singer on it.

Suggested Prompts

What do you do on different days of the week?

What kinds of decorations do you like on T-shirts?

Do you have a personal style?

What does your favorite T-shirt look like?

42. A letter to …

Related Topics

Friends and Family, Writing

Sample Language

Dear …

Sincerely, …

I'm writing because …

I wanted to tell you that …

Suggested Prompts

Who was the last person you wrote a letter or long email to?

Is there anyone you write to frequently?

Do you have something you would like to tell someone?

Is there a famous person you would like to write to?

43. An Act of Kindness

Related Topics

Thanksgiving, Friends and Family, Values

Sample Language

Once I needed help because …

I had a problem.

I was so grateful.

It meant a lot to me because …

Suggested Prompts

When was the last time someone did something kind for you?

Who is the kindest person you know?

What's an act of kindness you will never forget?

Have you ever had a difficult time and someone helped you?

44. Rewind to the Best Day Ever

Related Topics

Holidays, Tourism, Travel, Hobbies

Sample Language

One year ago, …

This happened in New York.

It the best day because …

The first thing that happened was …

I was with my sister and my cousin.

Suggested Prompts

What was the happiest day of your life?

What was the most interesting thing you've ever done?

Have you ever done something you've always wanted to do?

What was the best trip or vacation you've ever had?

45. The Ultimate Top

Related Topics

Clothes, Shopping, Art

Sample Language

My top is made of wool/cotton/ polyester/cashmere.

It always fits no matter what.

I like bright and colorful sweaters.

Suggested Prompts

Do you have a favorite sweater?

What's your favorite color?

Do you have a personal style?

46. Adventure Awaits

Related Topics

Goals, Achievements, Hobbies, Tourism

Sample Language

One thing I want to do is …

I want to learn how to …

Going to California is on my list because …

Suggested Prompts

If you could go anywhere in the world, where would you go?

What's something you've always wanted to do?

Is there something you want to learn to do?

Is there a person you'd like to meet?

47. I did it

Related Topics

Goals, Emotions

Sample Language

I'm so proud that I finally …

The hardest thing I ever did was …

I felt so proud …

My family told me …

Suggested Prompts

What's an achievement you are proud of?

What's something you worked hard at and finally achieved?

Do you have a future goal?

48. Make a Wish

Related Topics

Goals

Sample Language

I wish for …

I would like to …

I wish I could …

I wish I had …

Suggested Prompts

What's something you hope will happen soon?

What's a problem you have that you want to solve?

If you could have anything in the world, what would it be?

49. Nicknames

Related Topics

About Myself

Sample Language

My dad calls me … because …

My soccer team calls me …

Friends call me …

I like the name …

Suggested Prompts

Do your friends or family call you a special name?

Do you want a different name?

What are the names of your favorite characters from movies, TV, or a book?

How do people get nicknames in your culture?

50. These are My Favorite Things

Related Topics

About Myself

Sample Language

My favorite book is …

My favorite teacher is … because …

I love baseball.

The best teacher is … because …

Suggested Prompts

What are your favorite things (book, song, color, smell, food, teacher, hobby)?

Do you have any things that remind you of people you care about?

Do you have any souvenirs from a place you've been?

Is there a device you use a lot and have a favorite kind of?

51. My Rhyming Poem

Related Topics

Poetry, Creative Writing

Sample Language

Varies

Suggested Prompts

List some words that rhyme.

Do you have a favorite poem?

Do you know any poets who write in rhyme?

52. Favorite Things to Do in the …

Related Topics

Hobbies, Activities, Seasons

Sample Language

I like skiing in the winter.

In the fall, I always go walking in the woods.

Summer is the best time to go swimming.

Suggested Prompts

What are your favorite activities to do in different seasons?

What are your hobbies? When do you do these activities?

What do you like about each season?

Is there something you love doing but can only do at certain times of the year?

What are your favorite holidays and when do they occur?

53. A Book About Me

Related Topics

About Me

Sample Language

If there were a book about me, it would be called …

My book would be about …

I want to write a book about …

Suggested Prompts

If someone wrote a book about you, what would it be about?

What's something you wish everyone knew about you?

Do you have a story about your life you always tell?

54. My Robot

Related Topics

Inventions, Technology

Sample Language

My robot can …

My robot uses nuclear energy.

My robot's name is …

My robot helps me …

The computer goes here, and it helps the robot …

Suggested Prompts

Is there something you dislike doing?

Is there something you wish you could have any time?

What parts will your robot have?

55. My Goals

Related Topics

Goals, Jobs

Sample Language

I want to …

I hope someday to …

My life goal is to …

Suggested Prompts

Think of one goal for school, one goal for your family life, and one goal for your .

What's something you want to learn how to do?

What do you hope to do by the end of this class?

56. My Superpower

Related Topics

About Me, Everyday Routines

Sample Language

The superpower I want is …

I wish I could fly/had super strength/could turn invisible.

I'm really good at … so it's like a superpower.

Suggested Prompts

If you could have any super power, real or imaginary, what would it be?

What's something you are really good at?

Do you have a favorite superhero?

57. My Awesome Cool Invention

Related Topics

Inventions, Technology

Sample Language

My invention is a new Virtual Reality device.

This part makes it go faster.

It makes me snacks like this …

You control it by …

Suggested Prompts

Is there a task you hate doing?

Is there something you want any time you want?

Think of something you own worked better?

58. The Best Part of my Age

Related Topics

About Me, Society

Sample Language

I love being a kid because …

I can't wait to be a teenager so I can …

Old people are great because …

Suggested Prompts

What are the advantages of being a child, a teenager, an adult, and an older person?

Is there any age you look forward to being?

Is childhood the best part of your life?

Are you excited to grow up?

59. What Can You Teach Others?

Related Topics

About Me

Sample Language

I'm good at …

One thing I learned is that …

My favorite fun fact is …

Once I taught someone …

Suggested Prompts

What is something you are really good at?

What's an activity you've done for a long time?

Is there a topic you like to read about?

60. What's in a Name?

Related Topics

About Me, Vocabulary

Sample Language

I like … because …

This is my favorite word …

Suggested Prompts

What are the letters in your name?

What are some things you like that begin with that letter?

About This Book

What makes you smile? When do you feel good about yourself, your family, and the world? What can you do to help students enjoy learning more in school?

I loved school as a child; I loved learning and sharing. The positive atmosphere in the schools I attended celebrated learning, encouraged me, and helped me grow as a person. This book sets out to do just that with 60 positive activities. Yet these positive classroom activities have a serious purpose: facing academic challenges with more acceptance, building a sense of resilience, and encouraging mindfulness.

Take a few minutes to remember your past positive emotions. Savor them. How do you feel now?

Sometimes we, as teachers and parents, get caught in a negative cycle. However, research shows that frustration and dissatisfaction often worsen memory processing and learning efficiency in children. The prompts in this book are designed to help free students from this negativity by encouraging students to build self-understanding, find meaning, and create compassion.

Most of these activities take the form of a short writing prompt. However, it is also possible to ask students to make drawings or discuss the prompt with a partner. These reflective activities show students how to explore their creativity through visualization and self-expression. You may also choose to adapt these flexible exercises to fit your curriculum in a variety of ways.

Some students may want to collect their responses. They can use them to start discussions or explore possibilities with their friends and family. Other students may be hesitant to write for fear of others discovering and reading their responses as some of the activities can be quite personal, like a diary or journal. You may want to allow students to dispose of their writings after they have written the day's entry. No one need ever to see what they've written. The process of self-expression is fruitful even if the text is immediately destroyed. Creation can be its own reward.

How to Use This Book

This book was intentionally created to fit into the classroom in a variety of ways: as a daily activity, as a do-now, as a prompt for a longer piece, as a filler, as a fast-finisher, or an end of class activity. The application possibilities are endless. Use – and trust – your own judgment.

Here are sample directions that you can use with your students:

1. Set a timer or stopwatch for 10 minutes. In this time, think about the best possible situation for the prompt and respond in the space provided. You may want to respond with notes, sentences, or a drawing.

2. If writing, grammar or punctuation may not be the focus. Expressing your thoughts and emotions is key. Your ideas matter most.

3. After completing the activity, you can reflect on your feelings and answer. Think about the following questions:

   - **What effects did this activity have?**

   - **Does this exercise affect you more emotionally, mentally, physically, or spiritually?**

   - **Did it motivate or inspire you?**

   - **Does it encourage you to make changes?**

   - **How did this activity affect you overall?**

4. If using this activity as a prompt or pre-writing exercise, you can go back and edit or work with your response.

We hope you have as much of a wonderful, positive experience using it as we did creating it. Thank you!

THE BEST THINGS IN LIFE ARE FREE

CONSULTANT _____

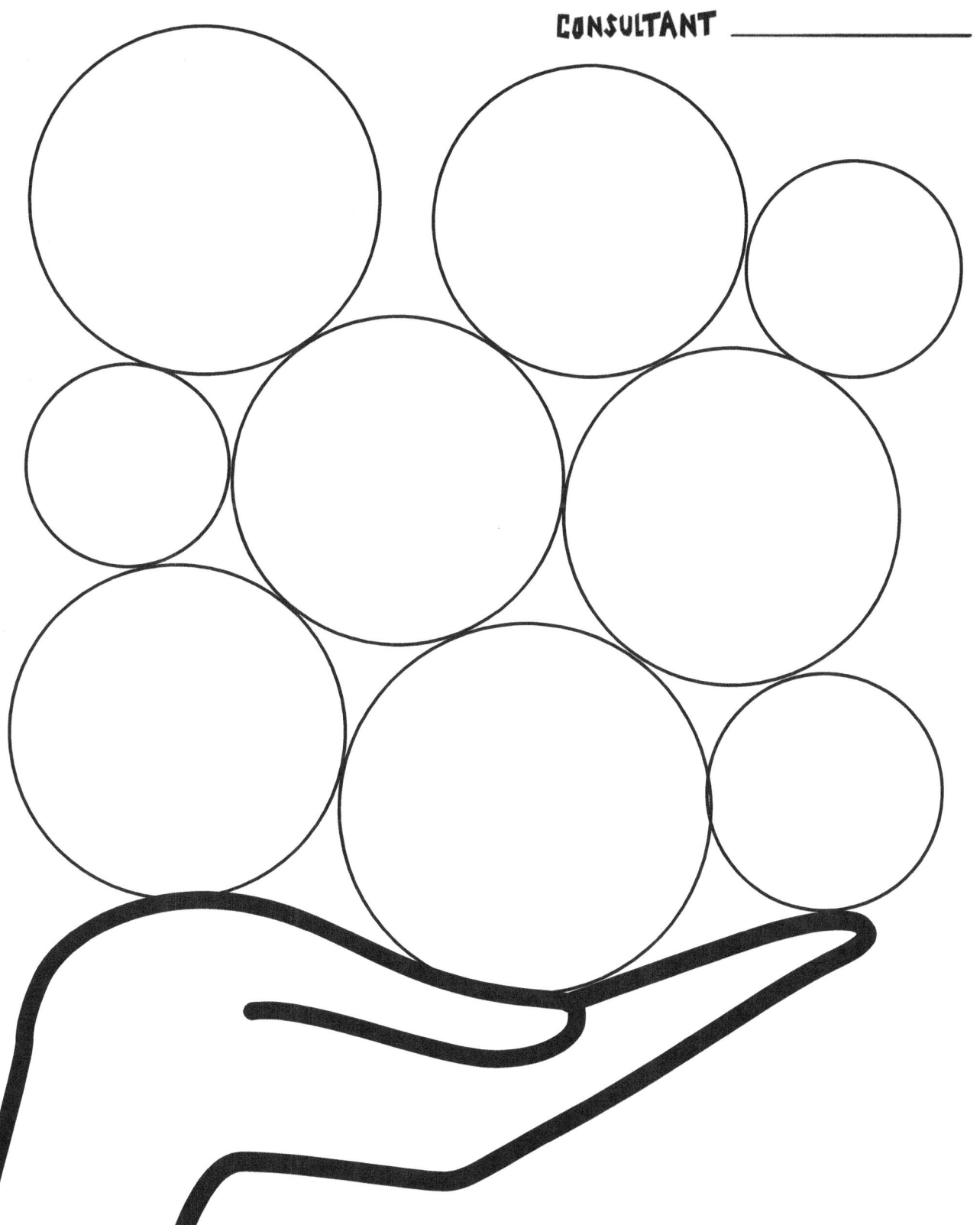

QUICK WAYS TO MAKE ME LAUGH

WRITE A THANK YOU NOTE TO SOMEONE WHO HAS HELPED YOU RECENTLY

DEAR _____,

_____

_____

_____

_____

_____

_____

_____

_____

_____

THANK YOU!

SINCERELY,

_____

A FUNNY PHOTO

PHOTOGRAPHER_____

ASTRONAUT _____

WHAT WOULD YOUR PLANET LOOK LIKE?

DREAM HOME

ENGINEER _____

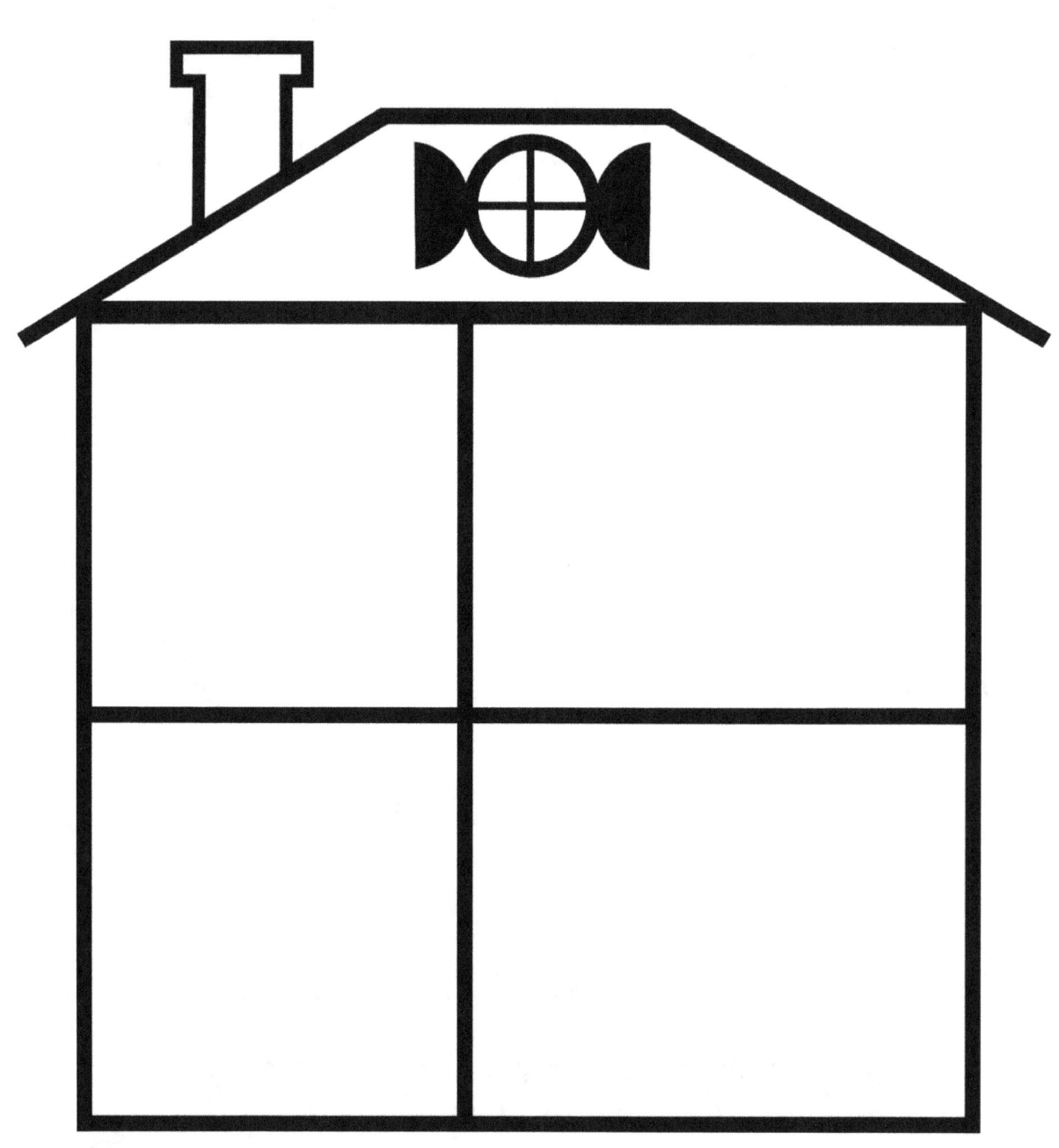

MY ADVICE ABOUT LIFE

COACH _____

SILLY JOKES I KNOW

COMEDIAN _____

A NEW FOOD CREATION

CHEF _____

I LAUGHED SO HARD WHEN ...

A DREAM THAT CAME TRUE...

DREAMER _____

COLORS THAT MAKE ME HAPPY

A HAPPY MESSAGE IN THE SKY

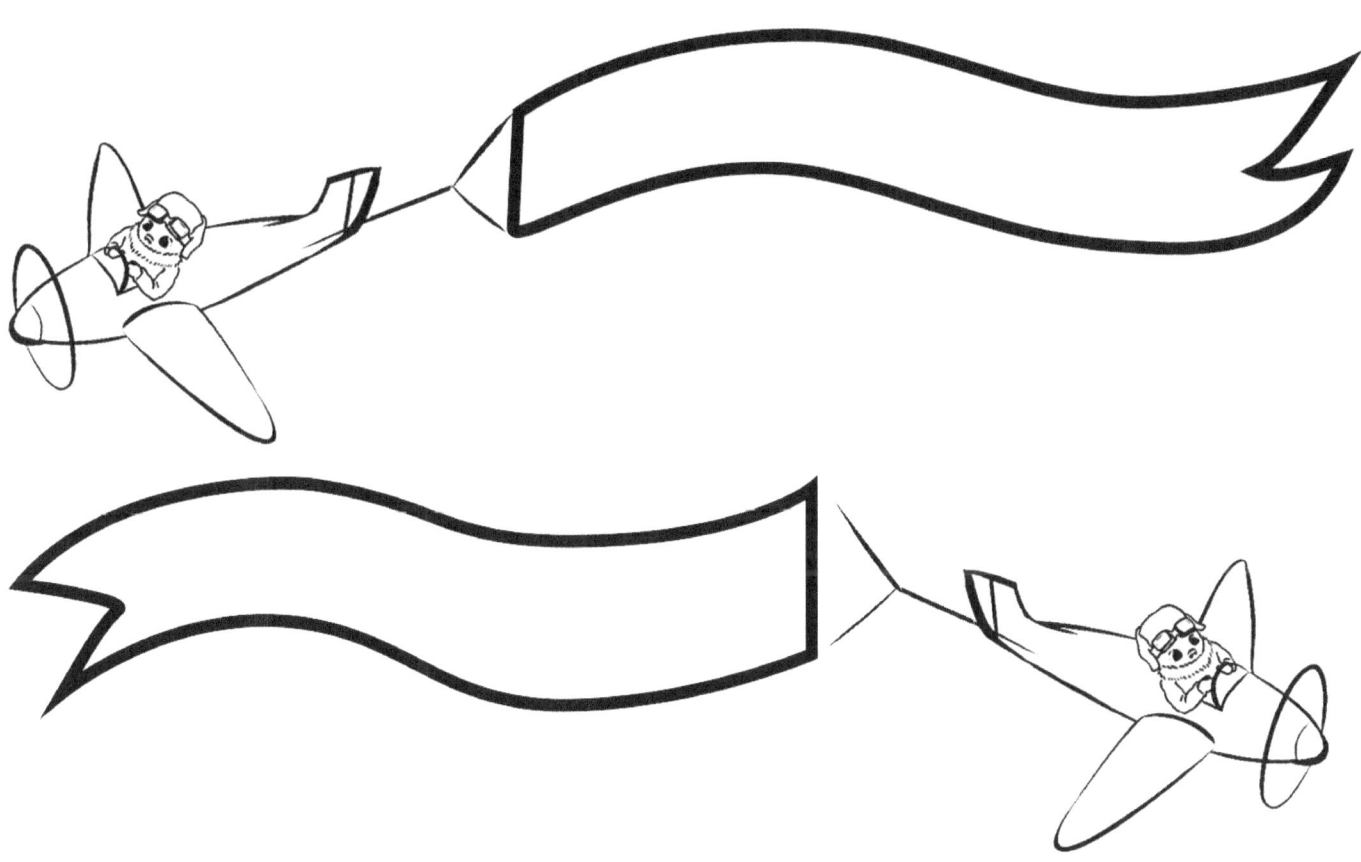

WHAT IS YOUR FAVORITE MEMORY?

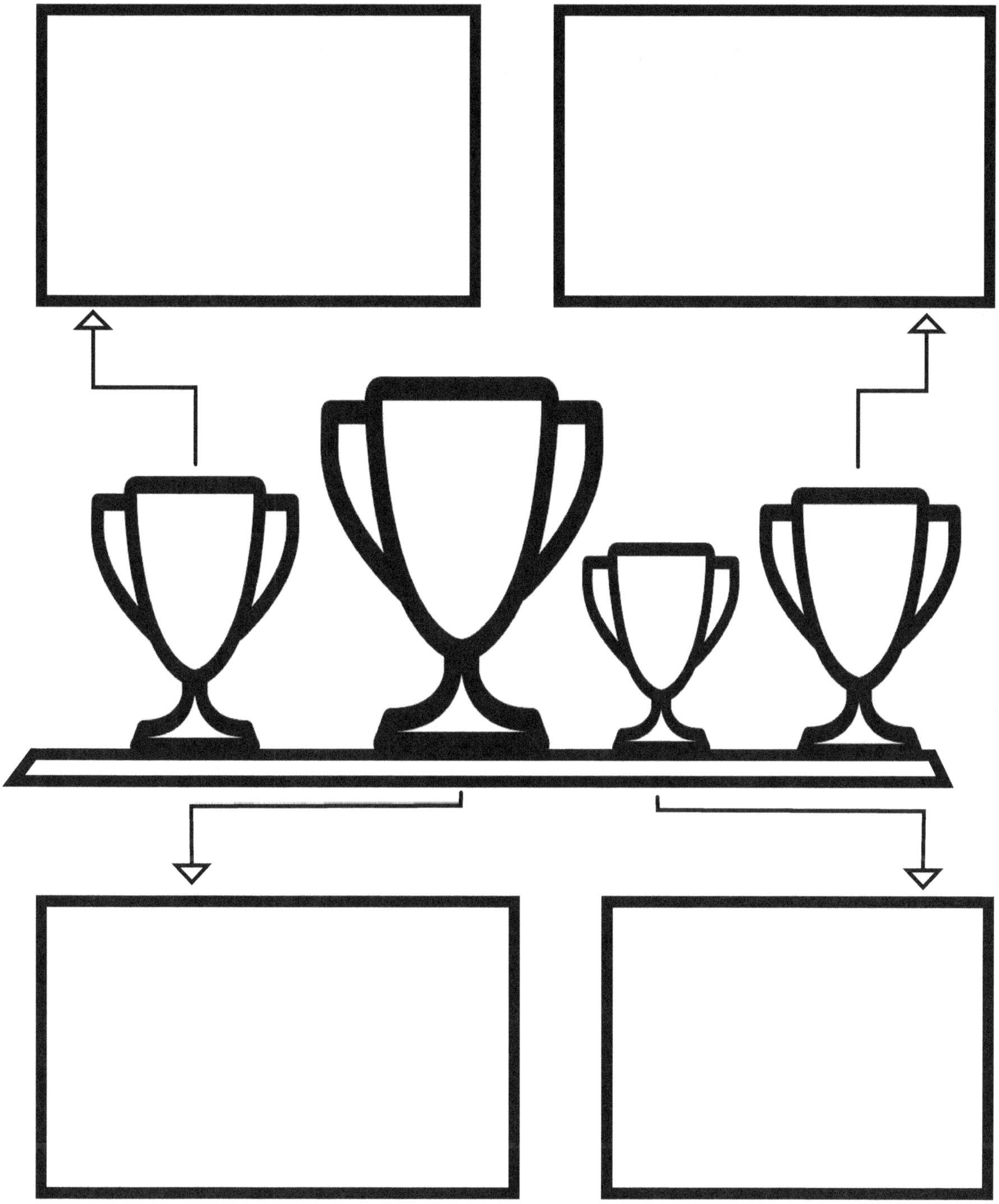

WINNER _____

GOOD THINGS I'VE DONE

BIG OR SMALL

#SELFIE

THE PEOPLE OF MY LIFE

I AM SPECIAL BECAUSE ...

2 _____

1 _____

3 _____

4 _____

6 _____

5 _____

60 Positive Activities for Kids © 2019 Teresa X. Nguyen and Tyler Hoang

A PRESENT TO MYSELF

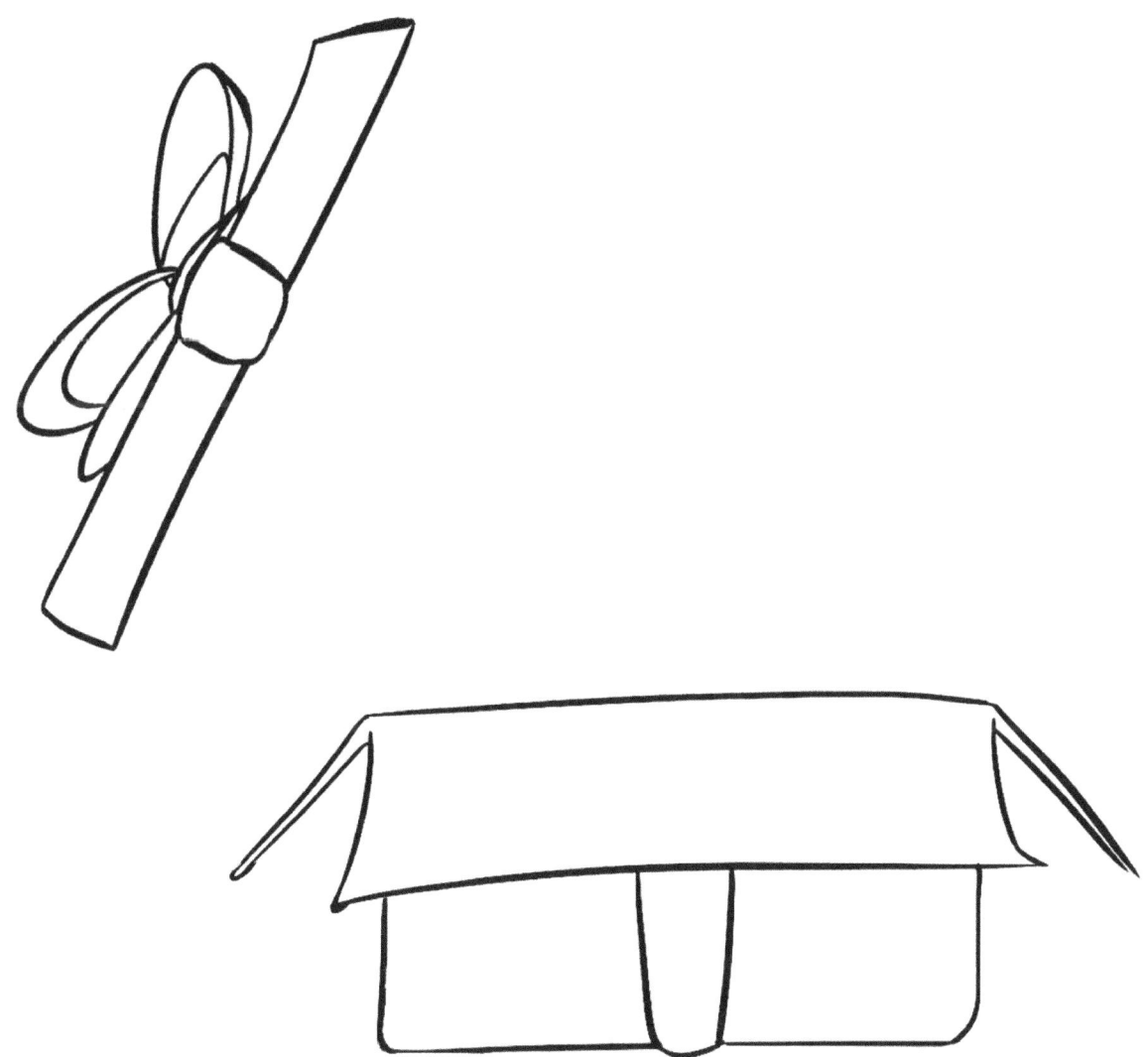

GIVER _____

AN ENJOYABLE CONVERSATION

THE FUTURE IS IN YOUR HANDS!

WRITE A FORTUNE FOR EACH COOKIE

FORTUNE TELLER _____

CREATE YOUR OWN MOVIE

DIRECTOR _____

DJ _____

#1 SONG

CHOOSE LYRICS FROM YOUR FAVORITE SONG TO CREATE A WHOLE NEW SONG!

WHAT IS YOUR HAPPY SMELL?

A RULE EVERYONE SHOULD FOLLOW

LAW MAKER _____

CONGRATULATIONS TO ME

CONGRATULATIONS

AWARDED TO

_____

FOR

_____

_____ DATE   SIGNATURE _____

#THANKFUL

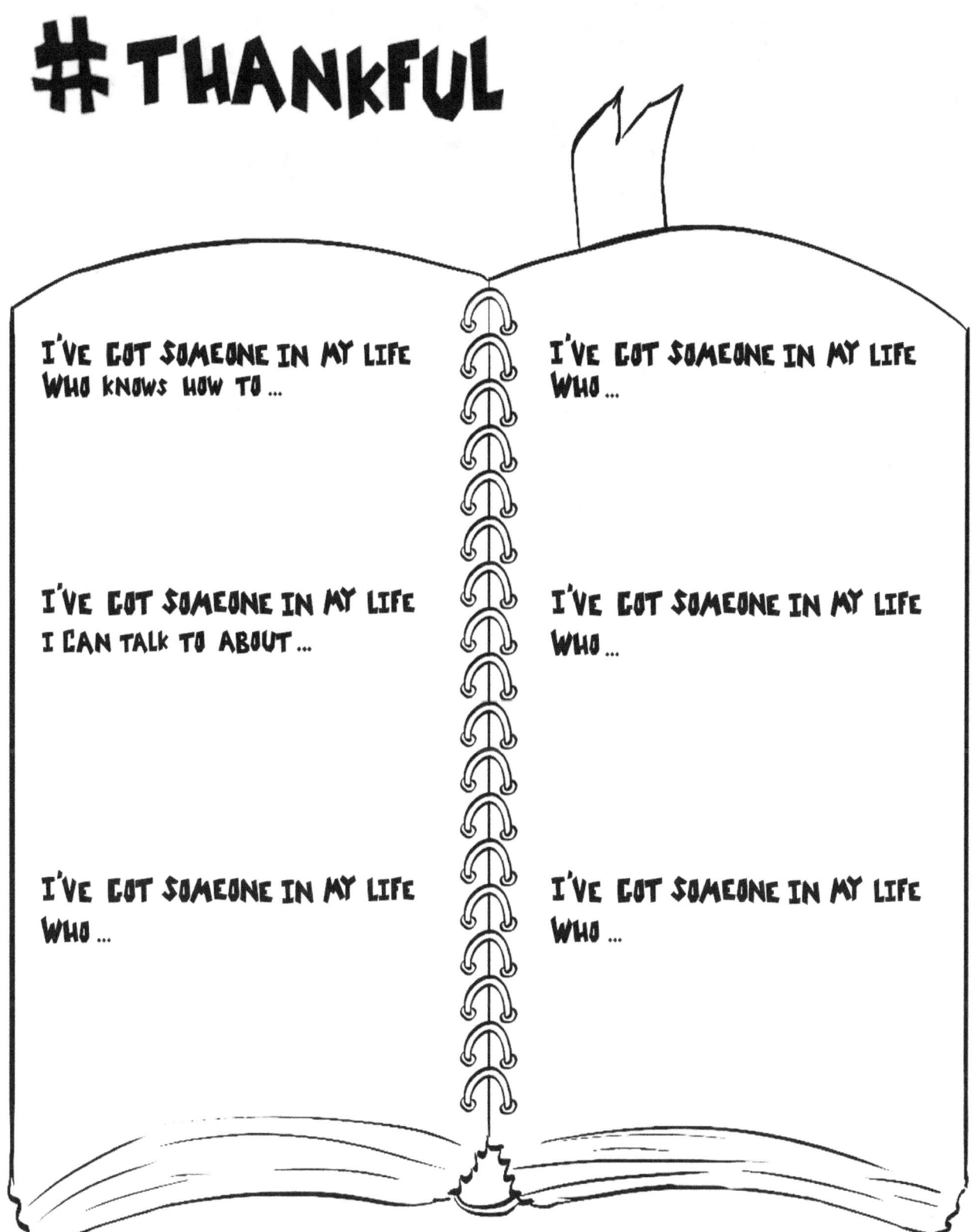

I'VE GOT SOMEONE IN MY LIFE
WHO KNOWS HOW TO ...

I'VE GOT SOMEONE IN MY LIFE
WHO ...

I'VE GOT SOMEONE IN MY LIFE
I CAN TALK TO ABOUT ...

I'VE GOT SOMEONE IN MY LIFE
WHO ...

I'VE GOT SOMEONE IN MY LIFE
WHO ...

I'VE GOT SOMEONE IN MY LIFE
WHO ...

SOUVENIRS FROM THE ADVENTURES I'VE BEEN ON

HAPPY PERSON ____________

I'M HAPPY WHEN ____________

I'M HAPPY WHEN ____________

I'M HAPPY WHEN ____________

I'M HAPPY WHEN ____________

I'M HAPPY WHEN ____________

I'M HAPPY WHEN ____________

I'M HAPPY WHEN ____________

I'M HAPPY WHEN ____________

I'M HAPPY WHEN ____________

I'M HAPPY WHEN ____________

I'M HAPPY WHEN ____________

I'M HAPPY WHEN ____________

I'M HAPPY WHEN ____________

I'M HAPPY WHEN ____________

I'M HAPPY WHEN ____________

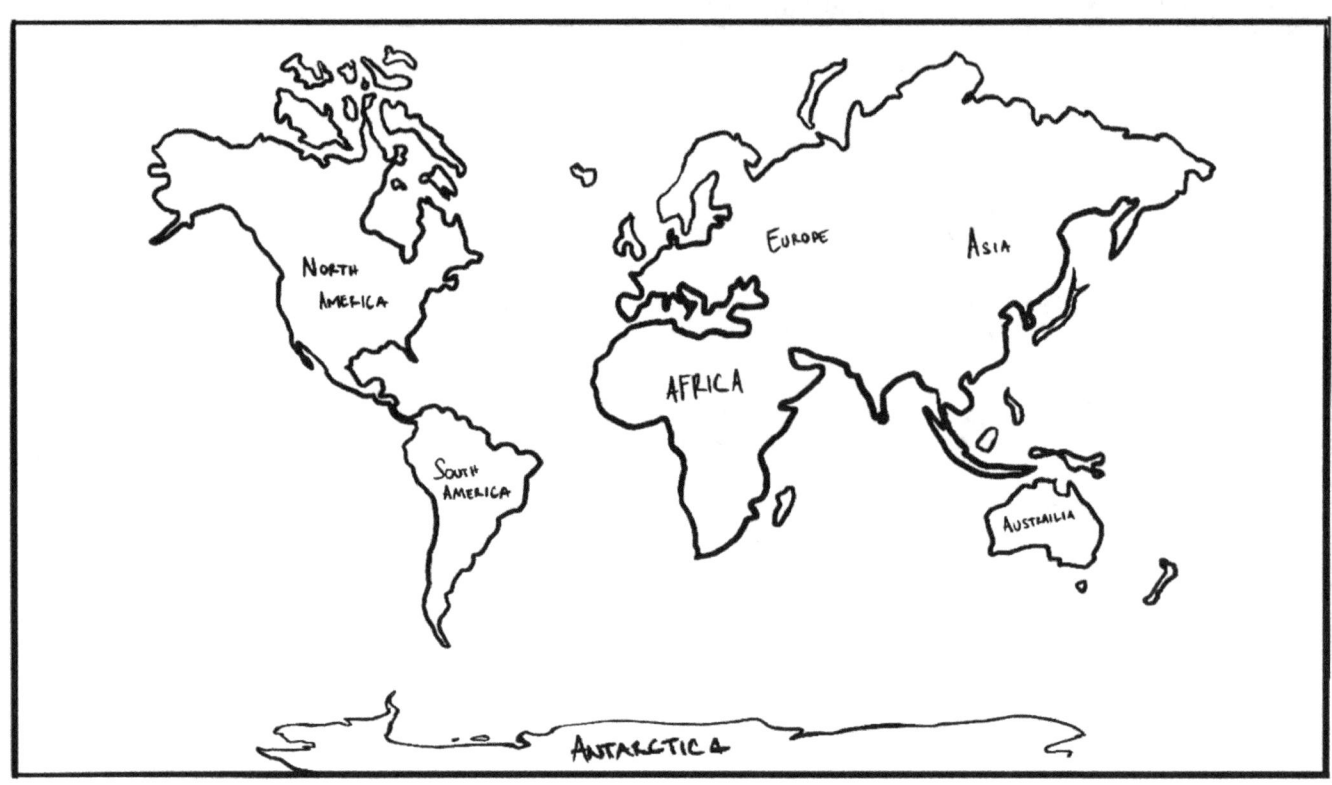

TOURIST _____

ALL THE PLACES I HOPE TO VISIT ONE DAY

SOME NEW EMOTIONS

CREATIONS _____

HAPPY

SHOCKED

GRUMPY

RANDOM MEMORY WITH SOMEONE I LOVE

SCRAPBOOKER _____

NEW HOLIDAY!

CREATE YOUR OWN HOLIDAY

WHAT WOULD YOU CELEBRATE?

HOW COULD YOU GET OTHERS TO JOIN IN THE EXCITEMENT?

HAPPY _____ Day

1	2	3	4	5	6	7
8	9	10	11	12	13	14
15	16	17	18	19	20	21
22	23	24	25	26	27	29
30	31					

WHAT IS _____ DAY?

ACTIVITES

TRADITIONS

FOOD!

RECENT MOMENTS OF JOY

THE BEST VACATION!

I SAW _____
I HEARD _____
I FELT _____
I SMELLED _____
I TASTED _____

HERO VS. ME

THIS IS HOW WE'RE ALIKE

MUSIC PLAYLIST

DJ _____

COMPLIMENTS I'VE RECEIVED

THE MOST BEAUTIFUL THING I'VE SEEN IN MY LIFE

BEAUTIFUL THING I SAW

FUN WORDS TO SAY

SUPER · CALI · FRAGI · LISTIC
EXPI · ALI · DO · CIOUS

DIS · COM · BOB · U
LA · TED

LOL · LY · GAG

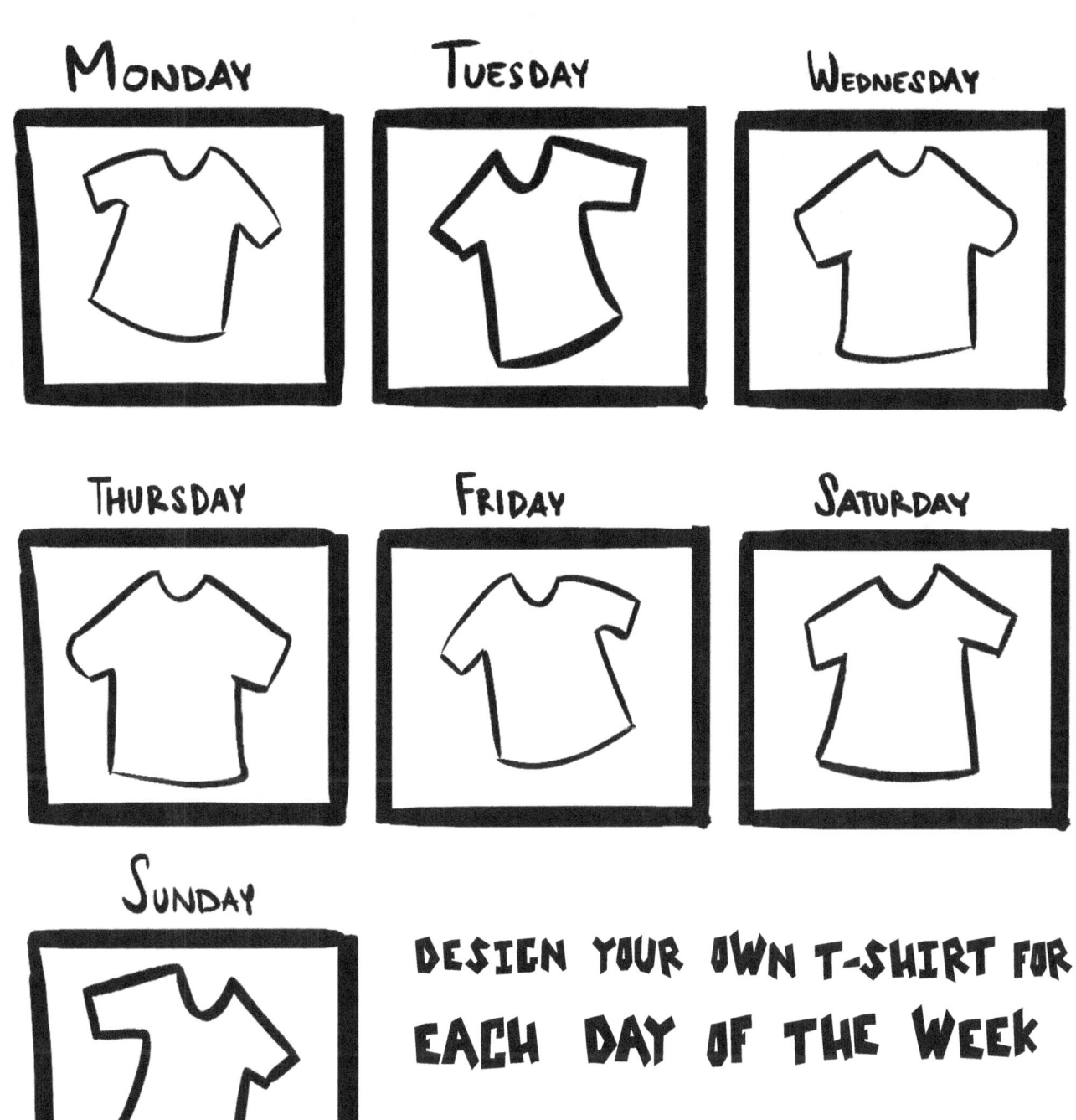

MONDAY

TUESDAY

WEDNESDAY

THURSDAY

FRIDAY

SATURDAY

SUNDAY

DESIGN YOUR OWN T-SHIRT FOR EACH DAY OF THE WEEK

A Letter to...

Dear _____,

Sincerely,

AN ACT OF
KINDNESS

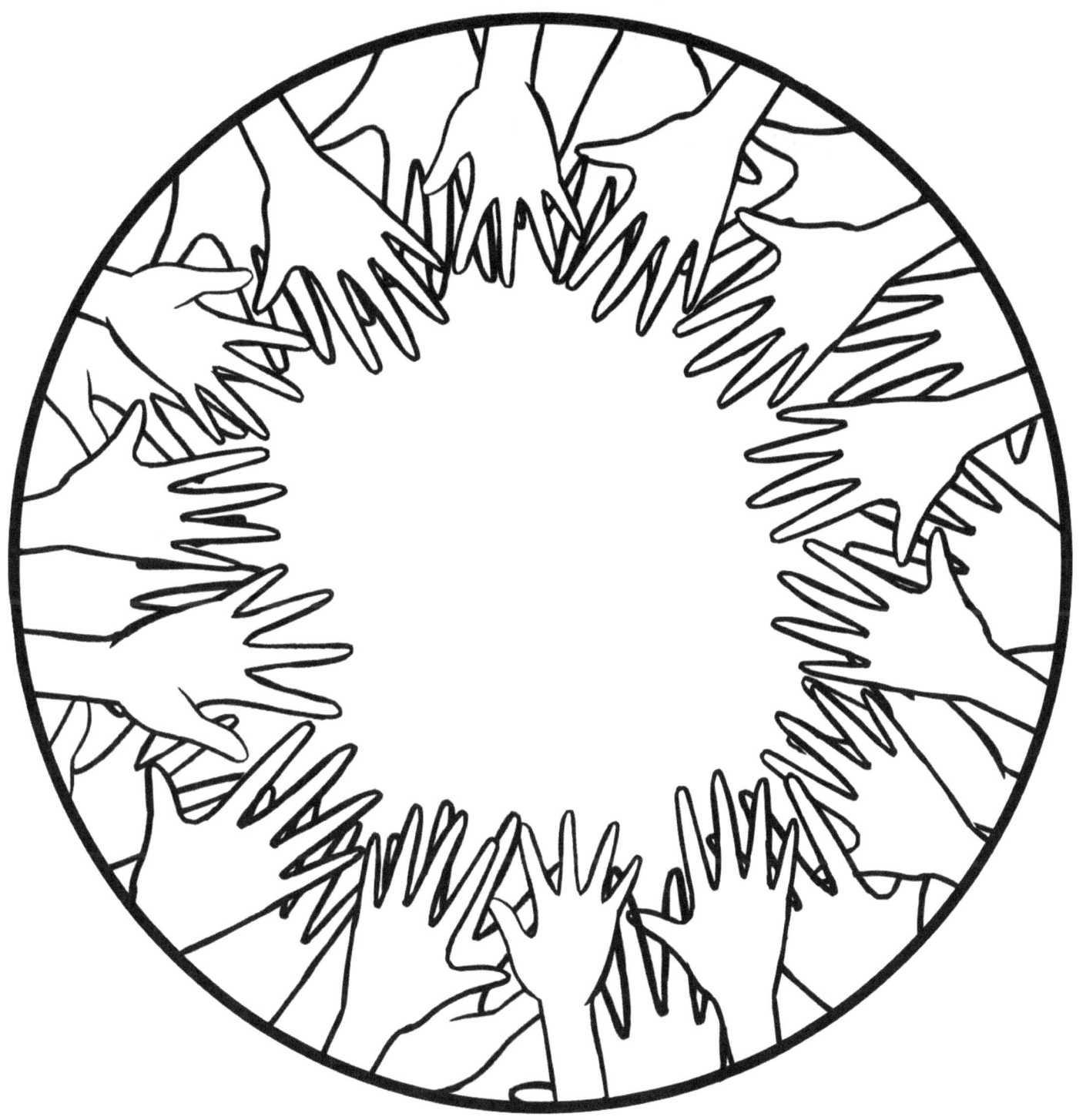

KIND PERSON _____

WRITE ABOUT A TIME WHEN SOMEONE HELPED YOU. HOW DID YOU FEEL AFTERWARD?

REWIND TO THE BEST DAY EVER

THE ULTIMATE TOP

WHAT DOES IT SMELL LIKE?

WHAT IS IT MADE OF?

OTHER FEATURES

DESIGNER _____

THINGS I WANT
TO DO IN MY LIFE

ADVENTURE
AWAITS!

ADVENTURER_____

I DID IT!

ACHIEVER _____

WRITE ABOUT A GOAL YOU ACCOMPLISHED RECENTLY.
HOW DID YOU FEEL WHEN YOU FINISHED IT?

MAKE A WISH

WISHER _____

NICKNAMES

HELLO! MY NAME IS...

HELLO! MY NAME IS...

HELLO! MY NAME IS...

HELLO! MY NAME IS...

MY FAVORITE THINGS

Book	
Song	
Color	
Smell	
Teacher	
Hobby	

MY RHYMING POEM

POET _____

FAVORITE THING TO DO IN THE ...

WINTER

SPRING

SUMMER

FALL

A BOOK ABOUT ME

TITLE

AUTHOR _____

MY ROBOT

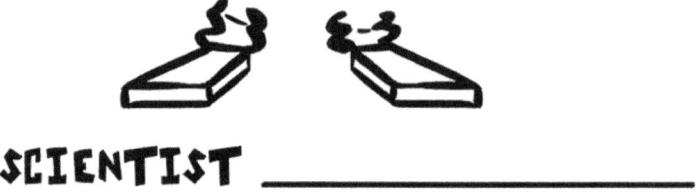

SCIENTIST _____

WHAT CAN YOUR ROBOT DO?

HOW CAN YOUR ROBOT STAY ALIVE?

WHAT IS YOUR ROBOT'S NAME?

MY GOALS

GOAL SETTER _____

MY SUPERPOWER

_____

SUPERHERO _____

MY AWESOME COOL
INVENTION

INVENTOR _____

THE BEST PART ABOUT BEING MY AGE IS

A _____
B _____
C _____
D _____
E _____
F _____
G _____
H _____
I _____
J _____
K _____
L _____
M _____

N _____
O _____
P _____
Q _____
R _____
S _____
T _____
U _____
V _____
W _____
X _____
Y _____
Z _____

WHAT CAN YOU TEACH OTHERS?

TEACHER _____

WHAT'S IN A...

WRITE YOUR NAME IN OUTLINE LETTERS AND FILL IN EACH LETTER
WITH WORDS YOU LIKE THAT BEGIN WITH THAT LETTER

About the Creators

Teresa X. Nguyen is a California-based content creator and teacher. She is the host and creator of *ESL Garage*, a bilingual YouTube channel for English-language learners and a co-author of the *Compelling Conversations* series.

Her classroom teaching, materials writing, and YouTube education projects reflect over ten years of teaching experience. Teresa has taught English-language learners from over twenty-five countries in China, Vietnam, and the United States. Her students have included a wide range from elementary school pupils to graduate students. She has an MA in Linguistics and a BA in English Literature.

A workaholic/workoutaholic by day and Korean-drama addict by night, she loathes writing in the third person but can be persuaded to do so every now and then. You can connect with Teresa at www.teresaxnguyen.com.

Tyler Hoang is a Digital Artist, animal lover, and camera enthusiast who lives between the Los Angeles and Orange Counties. He graduated from the California State University, Long Beach School of Art with a BFA in Animation/Illustration.

From sketching portraits to taking photographs, he never misses a beat when it comes to capturing a moment. Although he has poor eyesight, it doesn't faze his attention to detail.

Alongside dabbling in the arts, you can find him playing with his dog (or everyone else's), attempting to surf, or volunteering at his local church mentoring students.

Other Books by Alphabet Publishing

60 Positive Activies for Every Classroom
Teresa X. Nguyen and Nathaniel Cayanan

*Stories Without End: 24 open-ended stories to engage students
with reading, discussion, and creative writing*
Taylor Sapp

WWYD? 75+ Philosophical Dilemmas for Discussion
Taylor Sapp

Successful Group Work: 13 Activities to Teach Teamwork Skills
Patrice Palmer

50 Activities for the First Day of School
Walton Burns

Classroom Community Builders: Activities for the First Day & Beyond
Walton Burns

Browse our full catalogue at www.alphabetpublishingbooks.com. And while you're there, sign up for our mailing list to get free teaching tips, updates on our latest products, and discounts and giveaways you won't hear about anywhere else.